DISCOVERING GEOGRAPHY

THE WORLD

DAVID L. STIENECKER

■

ART BY RICHARD MACCABE

BENCHMARK BOOKS

MARSHALL CAVENDISH
NEW YORK

Benchmark Books
Marshall Cavendish Corporation
99 White Plains Road
Tarrytown, New York 10591

©Marshall Cavendish Corporation, 1998

Series created by Blackbirch Graphics, Inc.

Printed and bound in the United States.

Library of Congress Cataloging-in-Publication Data

Stienecker, David.
　　The world / by David L. Stienecker.
　　　　p.　　cm. — (Discovering geography)
　　Includes index.
　　Summary: Discusses the Earth and its natural features, climate, and products.
　　ISBN 0-7614-0543-7 (lib. bdg.)
　　1. Geography—Juvenile literature. [1. Earth. 2. Geography.]
I. Title. II. Series: Discovering geography (New York, N.Y.)
G133.S836　　1998
910—dc21

97-3017
CIP
AC

Contents

The Earth That Was

The Earth hasn't always looked like it does today. In fact, many scientists believe that about 180 million years ago the Earth was one large land-mass. They call it Pangaea. This map shows what Pangaea may have looked like. What is the name of the ocean that surrounds Pangaea?

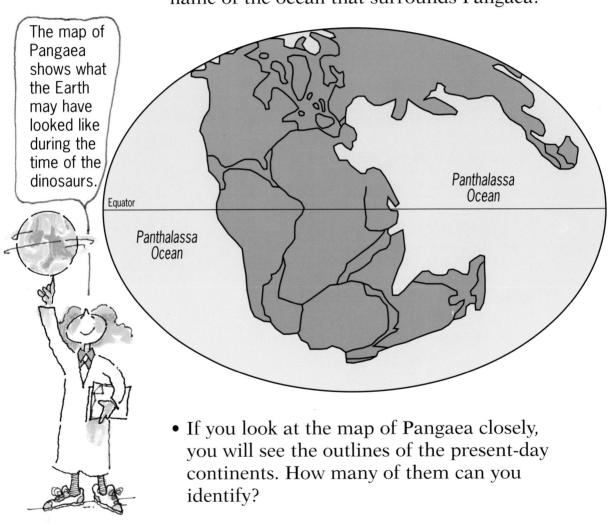

The map of Pangaea shows what the Earth may have looked like during the time of the dinosaurs.

Equator

Panthalassa Ocean

Panthalassa Ocean

• If you look at the map of Pangaea closely, you will see the outlines of the present-day continents. How many of them can you identify?

As time passed, Pangaea began to break up and drift apart. Eventually, the continents took on their present shape. The map below shows how the Earth may have looked about 60 million years ago. Can you identify the seven continents? Which landmass is not a continent?

Scientists believe that the Earth is about 4 1/2 billion years old!

- When you look at the maps, the continents seem to fit together like a puzzle. Make a puzzle by tracing or drawing each of the landmasses shown on the maps. Cut the pieces apart and mix them up. Then see if you can put them together to make Pangaea.

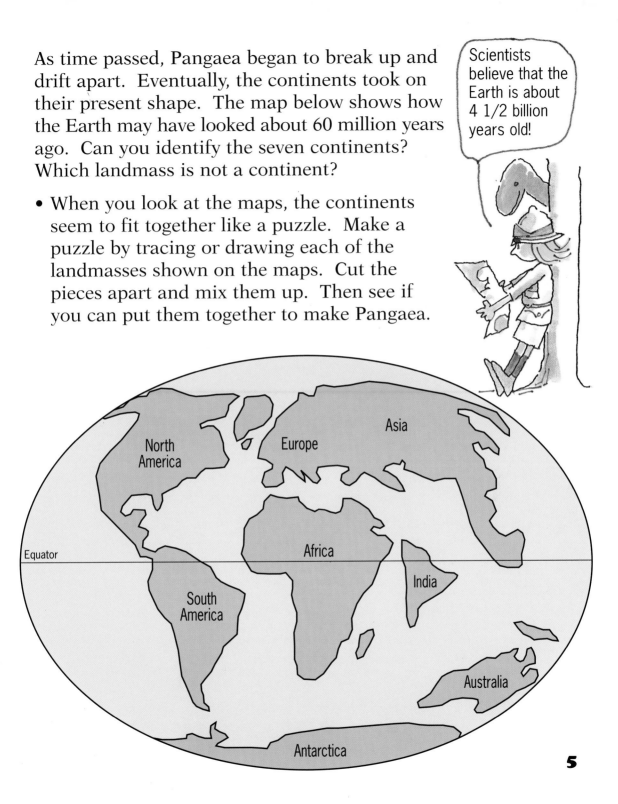

North America

Europe

Asia

Equator

Africa

India

South America

Australia

Antarctica

The Earth Today

This map shows what the Earth looks like today. Compare it to the map on the previous page that shows what the Earth looked like 60 million years ago. How has the Earth changed?

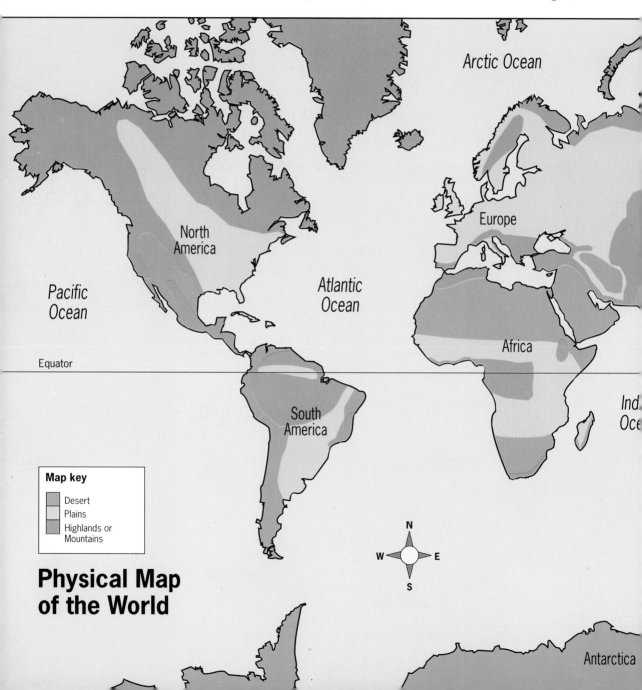

Arctic Ocean

Europe

North America

Pacific Ocean

Atlantic Ocean

Africa

Equator

South America

Ind. Oce

Map key

Desert

Plains

Highlands or Mountains

N
W E
S

Physical Map of the World

Antarctica

- See if you can locate and name each of the seven continents on the map.

- The map shows mountains, deserts, and plains. Locate each of these features on each of the continents.

Only about 30% of the Earth's surface is land; 70% is water.

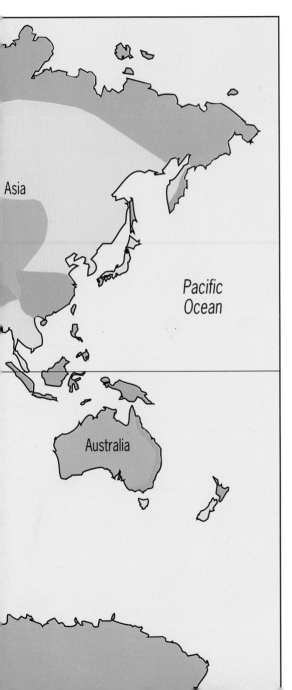

- Locate North America, the continent where you live. Compare it to one of the other continents. How are they alike? How are they different? Make a chart or fact sheet to compare the two continents.

- Play a game with a friend. Each player in turn gives a clue to a feature on the map. For example, "I'm a large body of water found between Africa and Asia. What am I called?" The other player must locate the feature on the map. If your partner is having trouble, give another clue.

The Earth on the Move

The Earth's surface is not one solid piece that never moves. The Earth's crust is actually made up of seven large plates and several smaller ones. Think of it as an egg with a cracked shell. The continents and oceans rest on top of these plates. The plates "float" on top of the Earth's molten outer core. As the plates move, the continents and oceans move with them.

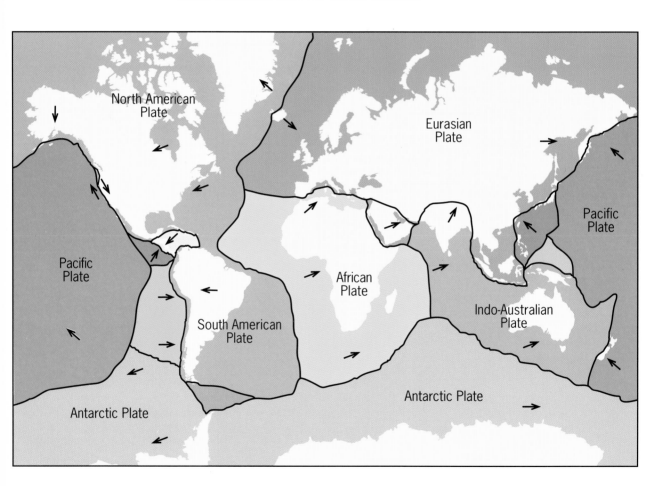

The map shows the shapes and locations of the Earth's tectonic plates. The arrows show the direction in which the plates move. Locate and identify the seven major plates. What do these seven plates remind you of?

- Locate where you live on the map. What is the name of the tectonic plate you are living on? What are the names of the plates that border it?

- You can think of the Earth as a giant jigsaw puzzle with seven very large pieces. Make the jigsaw puzzle pieces by tracing the seven major plates and cutting them out. Then see how they fit together.

- Compare the map on page 8 to the maps on the previous pages. Now that you know about the Earth's tectonic plates, how could you use that information to explain how the surface of the Earth has changed?

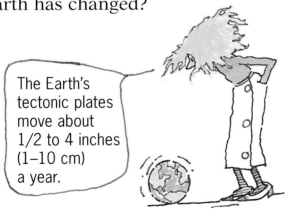

The Earth's tectonic plates move about 1/2 to 4 inches (1–10 cm) a year.

Hot, Cold, and In Between

This map shows some of the Earth's temperature regions. Each color shows a different temperature range. To find out what the temperature is like in a particular part of the world, just look at the map key.

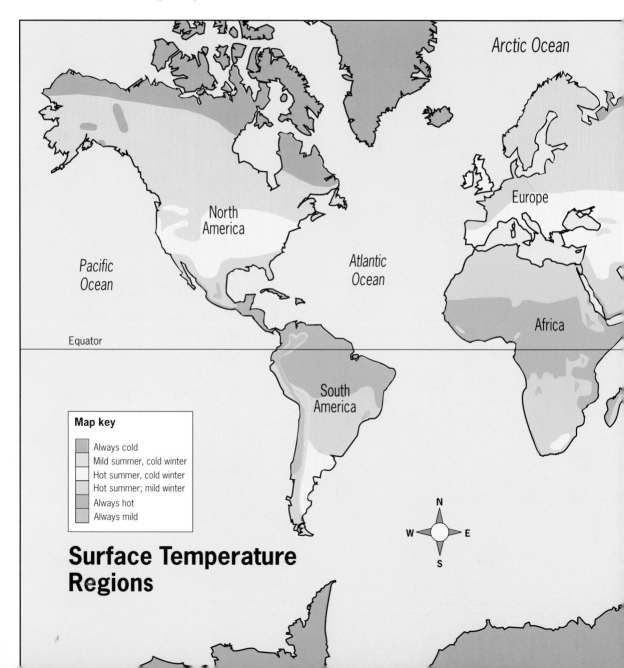

Arctic Ocean

Europe

North America

Pacific Ocean

Atlantic Ocean

Africa

Equator

South America

Map key

Always cold
Mild summer, cold winter
Hot summer, cold winter
Hot summer; mild winter
Always hot
Always mild

Surface Temperature Regions

N
W E
S

- Locate the area of the United States in North America. What are the different temperature regions in the United States?

- The Earth's temperature regions appear like bands that encircle the globe. Describe the temperature regions you would pass through as you traveled from the northernmost regions to the equator.

You can play a game using this map and the physical map of the world on pages 6–7. Here's what to do:

- Write the names of several natural features on index cards—deserts, plains, and so on. Turn the cards over and mix them up.

- Each player in turn draws a card, points to the feature on the physical map, and identifies the temperature region(s) where it is located.

- If the player cannot identify the temperature region, the card is returned to the pile.

- If the player identifies the temperature region(s), he or she keeps the card. The player with the most cards at the end of the game wins.

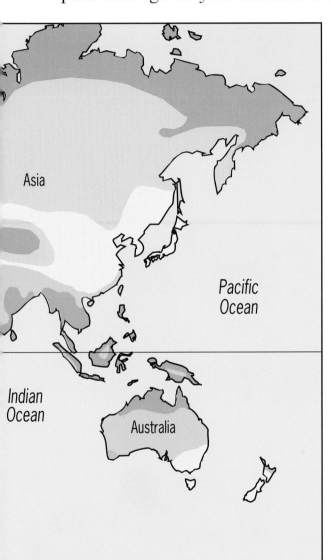

Climates Around the World

If you were traveling to a certain part of the world, you might like to know what the climate is like. You could get some idea by looking at a climate map. This climate map shows four different kinds of climates.

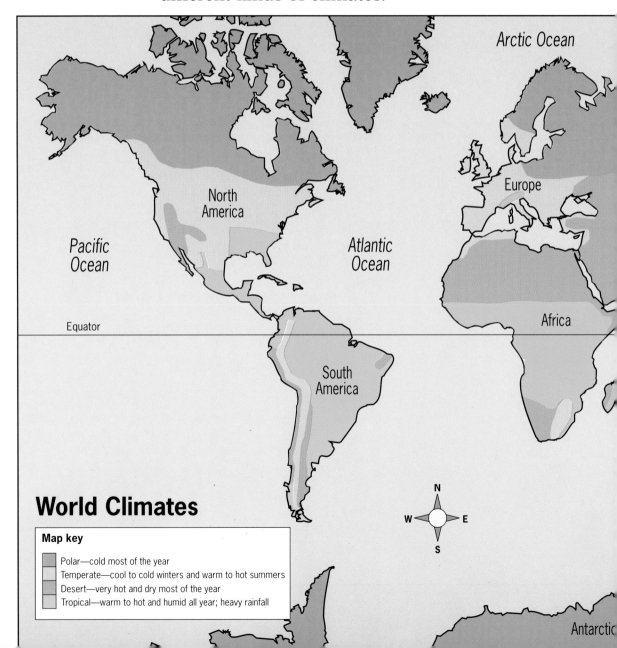

World Climates

Map key

Polar—cold most of the year
Temperate—cool to cold winters and warm to hot summers
Desert—very hot and dry most of the year
Tropical—warm to hot and humid all year; heavy rainfall

- Locate the area of North America on the map. What different climate regions are shown for North America?

- According to the map, which two continents have large areas of tropical climate?

- Locate Australia on the map. Imagine you are traveling across Australia from east to west. What climate areas would you pass through?

- Compare the climates of North America to the climates of South America. How are they alike? How are they different?

- What is the climate of northern Asia like?

- What is the climate of most of Europe?

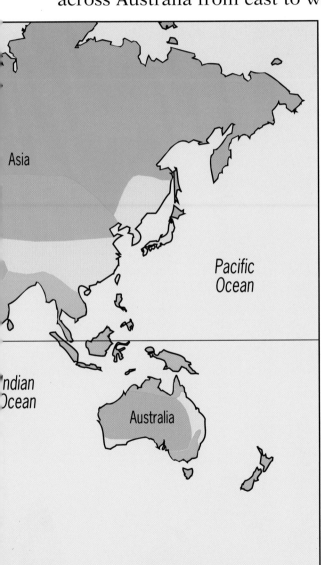

Asia

Pacific Ocean

Indian Ocean

Australia

Climate is the average weather of a place over a long period of time.

How People Use the Land

This map shows how the people of the world use the land. The colors on the map tell you what most of the people do for a living in that part of the world. The map key can help you figure out what the colors mean.

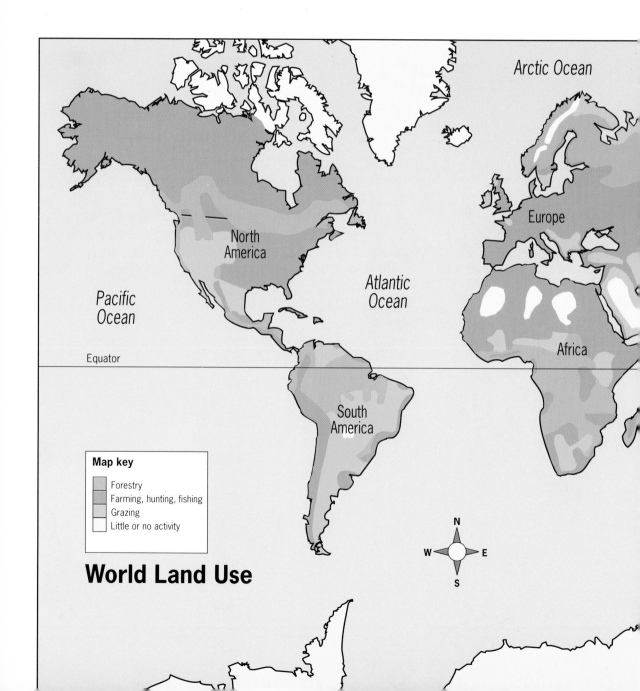

Arctic Ocean

Europe

North America

Atlantic Ocean

Pacific Ocean

Africa

Equator

South America

Map key

Forestry
Farming, hunting, fishing
Grazing
Little or no activity

World Land Use

N
W E
S

- What color would tell you where most of the people grow farm crops for a living?

- What color would tell you where logging occurs?

- The land in the United States is used many different ways. According to the map, how is much of the land in the United States used?

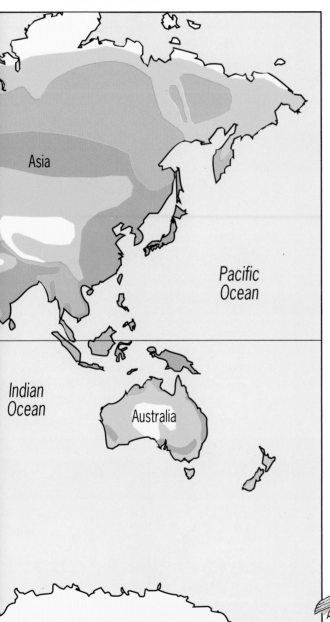

Asia

Pacific Ocean

Indian Ocean

Australia

Antarctica

- Locate four parts of the world in which farming is the main way people use the land. Use direction words and the names of continents to describe where these places are.

- Where in the world is there little or no activity on the land? Why do you think this is true for these parts of the world?

A natural resource is a product that comes from the Earth that people need or use.

15

Foods from Around the World

Maps can be used to show where different kinds of food come from. This map shows ten different foods.

- You've probably eaten rice before. Which two countries on the map grow a lot of rice?

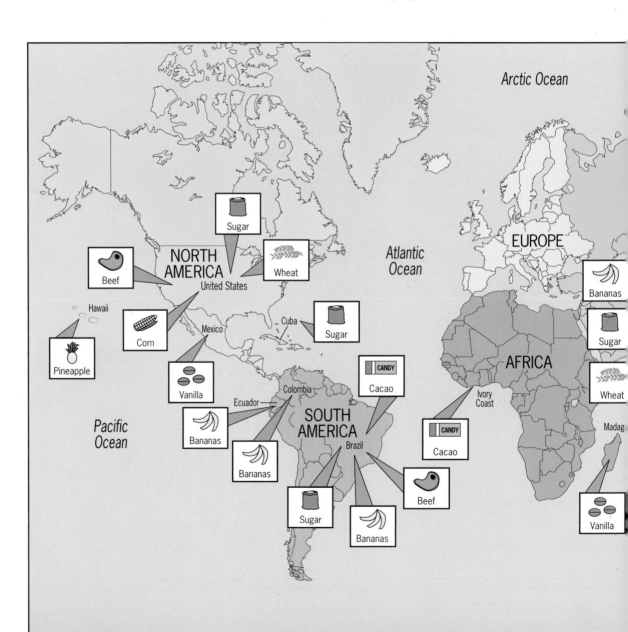

The next time you're in a supermarket, check to see where the rice they sell came from.

- Suppose you bought a chocolate-covered banana. Where might the banana have come from? Where might the chocolate have come from?

- The next time you go to a supermarket, see if they have pineapples. Check the label on one of the pineapples to see where it came from. Then check to see if the pineapple came from one of the places on the map.

- Keep track of the things you eat for a few days. Are any of them shown on the map? Where in the world did they come from?

- The United States grows more of one thing than any other country. Can you discover what it is by examining the map?

ASIA

Wheat

China

Rice

Pacific
Ocean

dia Pineapple

Coconut

Thailand

Philippines

Rice

I n d o n e s i a

Bananas

Vanilla

ndian
cean Coconut

AUSTRALIA

Cacao beans are used to make chocolate and cocoa.

17

World Energy Sources

We use energy to heat our homes, to provide us with electricity, to run our factories, and to keep cars on the highways. Maps like this one show where much of the world's energy resources come from.

The energy we use comes mainly from coal, natural gas, and petroleum.

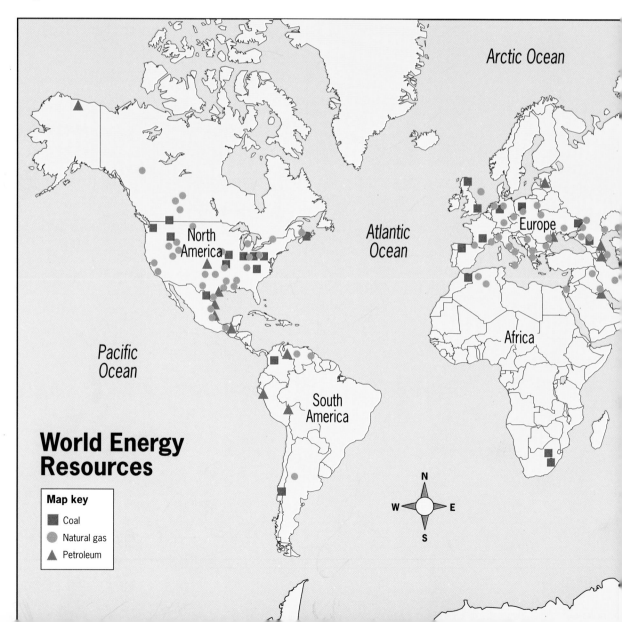

Arctic Ocean

North America

Atlantic Ocean

Europe

Africa

Pacific Ocean

South America

World Energy Resources

Map key
- ■ Coal
- ● Natural gas
- ▲ Petroleum

- Make a chart like the one below to show the energy resources for each continent.

CONTINENT	ENERGY RESOURCES
NORTH AMERICA	PETROLEUM, NATURAL GAS, COAL
SOUTH AMERICA	

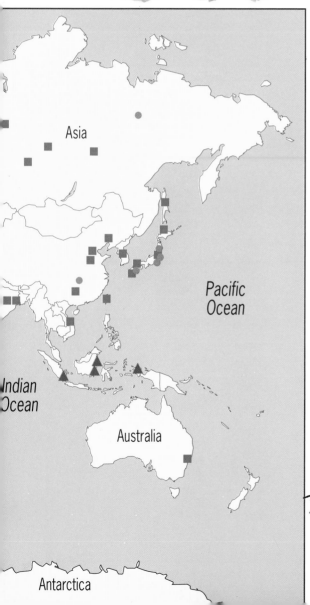

- Which of the energy resources shown on the map can be found in the United States?

- Which of the continents provide most of the world's energy resources? Which continents provide the least?

The United States uses more energy than any other country in the world.

Animal Travelers

Some animals travel great distances as they migrate from one place to another. This map shows the route of two of the world's greatest animal travelers. The Arctic tern migrates from the North Pole to the South Pole and back every year. The round trip is about 22,000 miles (35,400 kilometers)!

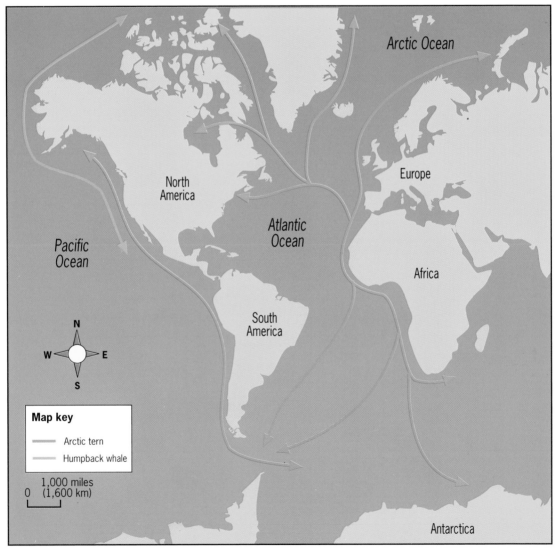

Arctic Ocean

North America

Europe

Atlantic Ocean

Pacific Ocean

Africa

South America

N
W   E
S

Map key
— Arctic tern
— Humpback whale

1,000 miles
0   (1,600 km)

Antarctica

- Use your finger to trace one of the migratory routes the Arctic tern takes. What continents does the route pass by?

- What ocean does some of the Arctic tern's migratory routes cross?

- What other animal's migratory route is shown on the map? How would you describe the route? Use the map scale to figure out about how many miles and how many kilometers this animal migrates.

Animals migrate to feeding grounds, better climates, and nesting sites.

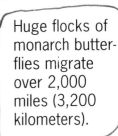

There are many animals that migrate long distances. Do some research to discover what some of them are. Make a map like the one on page 20 to show their migratory routes. Some animals you might want to check out are: monarch butterflies, European white storks, golden plovers, Canada geese, fur seals, cuckoos, swallows, and European eels.

Huge flocks of monarch butterflies migrate over 2,000 miles (3,200 kilometers).

Biomes of the World

A biome is a major area of the Earth with a certain kind of climate and where certain kinds of plants and animals live. This map shows several world biomes and where they are located. How many different biomes does the map show?

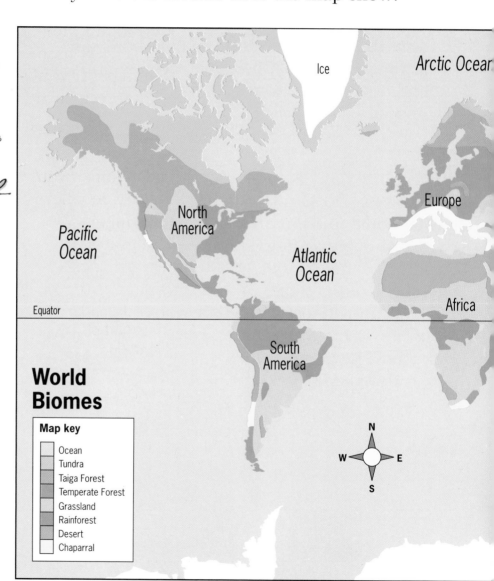

Tundra is treeless, harsh grassland. It has short, cool summers and long, cold winters.

Arctic Ocean

Ice

Europe

North America

Pacific Ocean

Atlantic Ocean

Africa

Equator

South America

World Biomes

Map key

- Ocean
- Tundra
- Taiga Forest
- Temperate Forest
- Grassland
- Rainforest
- Desert
- Chaparral

N
W E
S

- List four kinds of biomes you can find in the United States. Then locate about where you live on the map. What kind of biome is the area in which you live?

- Where are some of the major desert biomes in the world located? Use continent names and direction words to describe their locations.

- What are the names of the three forest biomes shown on the map? If you wanted to visit a rainforest, where might you go?

- Play a game. Close your eyes. Then touch the map with your finger. Open your eyes. Identify the biome where your finger is pointing.

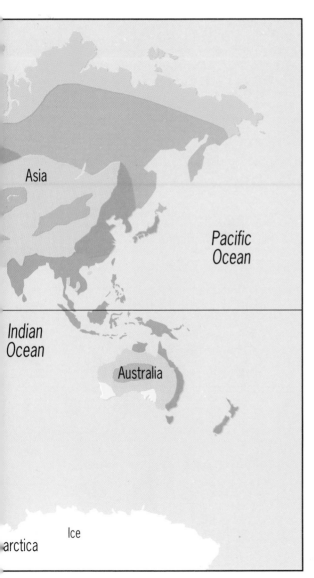

Asia

Pacific Ocean

Indian Ocean

Australia

Ice

arctica

A rainforest has more kinds of trees than any other part of the world.

Searching for Gems

You can make maps to show just about anything. For example, you might think of this map as a kind of treasure map. It shows where some of the world's most precious gems and minerals come from. Imagine traveling to one of these places and striking it rich!

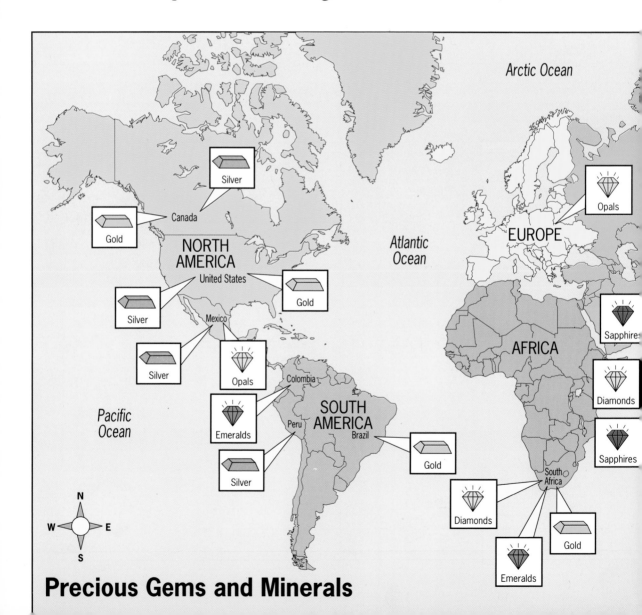

Precious Gems and Minerals

- Make a chart like this one to show which precious gems and minerals are found in which countries.

PRECIOUS GEM OR MINERAL	COUNTRY
EMERALDS	COLOMBIA, INDIA, SOUTH AFRICA, RUSSIA

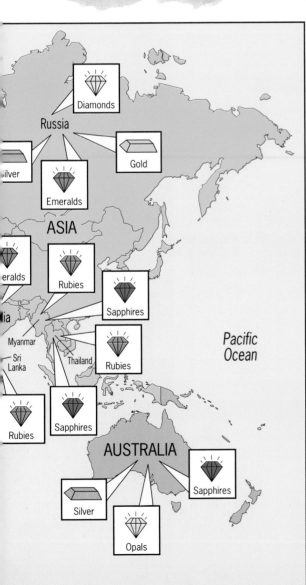

- If you wanted to look for gold, what countries would you go to? What countries would you go to for diamonds?

- If you traveled to Thailand, what gems would you find?

- Use the map to plan a treasure hunt. Decide which precious gems and minerals you would like to find. Then make a plan to travel to their locations.

Rubies are the rarest of all gems. Large ones are the most valuable gems in the world.

25

Where In the World?

Almost all the land in the world is divided up into countries or is owned by a country. This map of the world is called a political map. Some countries are labeled.

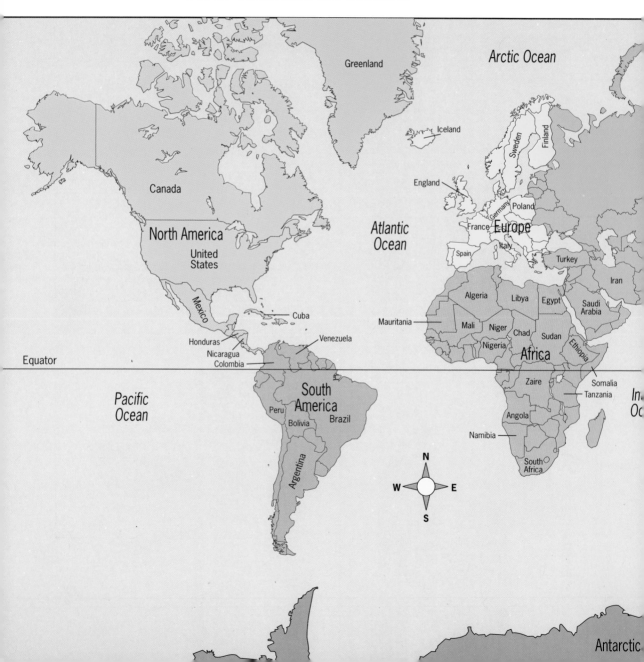

- Look at each country shape. Can you find which continent it belongs to and what the country name is?

You can trace shapes of other countries and ask a friend to name them and fit them into the right continent.

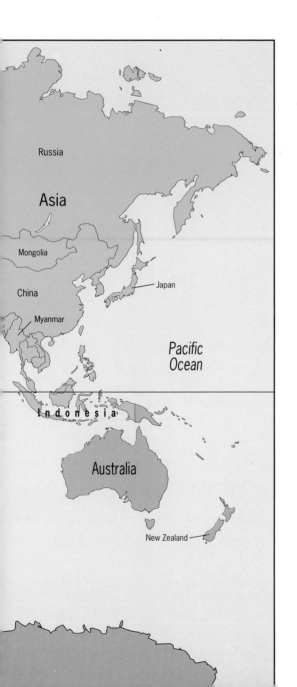

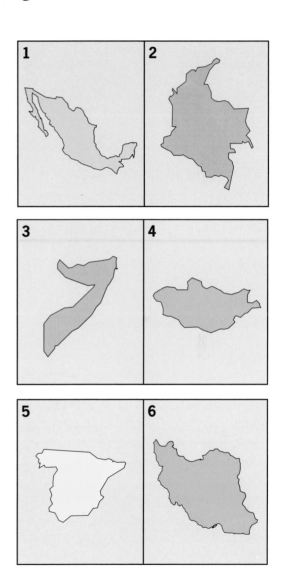

Answers

Pps. 4–5, The Earth That Was

The ocean surrounding Pangaea is called the Panthalassa Ocean.

The seven continents are North America, South America, Africa, Europe, Asia, Australia, and Antarctica. India is not a continent.

Pps. 6–7, The Earth Today

India has become attached to the Asian continent. North and South America have moved farther from Europe and Africa. Australia and Africa have moved north.

The seven continents are North America, South America, Africa, Europe, Asia, Australia, and Antarctica.

Pps. 8–9, The Earth on the Move

The seven major plates are: Pacific Plate, Eurasian Plate, North American Plate, African Plate, South American Plate, Indo-Australian Plate, Antarctic Plate. They are roughly the shapes of the seven continents.

You live on the North American Plate. It borders the Pacific Plate, the Eurasian Plate, and the African Plate.

The movement of tectonic plates has caused, and continues to cause, the surface of the Earth to change.

Pps. 10–11, Hot, Cold, and In Between

The U.S. temperature ranges are: mild summer, cold winter; hot summer, cold winter; hot summer, mild winter.

Always cold; mild summer, cold winter; hot summer, cold winter; hot summer, mild winter; always hot.

Pps. 12–13, Climates Around the World

Climate regions in North America include: desert, tropical, temperate, and polar.

Africa and South America have the largest areas of tropical climate.

Traveling from east to west in Australia you would pass through tropical or temperate climates, then deserts.

Both South America and North America have regions of temperate climate. South America has much more tropical climate. North America has much more temperate climate. Both continents have some desert.

Northern Asia has a polar climate.

Europe has a mostly temperate climate.

Pps. 14–15, How People Use the Land

Brown is the color used for growing farm crops.

Green is the color used for forestry use.

The land in the United States is used for forestry, grazing, and farming.

Farming occurs in the United States, Europe, northern Africa, and central Asia.

There is little or no activity in Antarctica and along the Arctic Ocean because the climate is too cold.

There is also little activity in hot desert regions in Australia, Africa, and Asia.

Pps. 16–17, Foods from Around the World

China and India produce large amounts of rice.

The banana might have come from Brazil, India, Colombia, Ecuador, or the Philippines. The chocolate may have come from the Ivory Coast or Brazil.

The United States grows more corn than any other place in the world.

Pps. 18–19, World Energy Sources

All of the energy sources on the map can be found in the United States.

North America: petroleum, coal, natural gas

South America: coal, petroleum, natural gas

Africa: coal, natural gas

Europe: coal, petroleum, natural gas

Asia: coal, petroleum, natural gas

Australia: coal

Antarctica: none

Pps. 20–21, Animal Travelers

The routes of the Arctic tern pass by the continents of North America, South America, Africa, Europe, and Antarctica.

Some of the Arctic tern's migratory routes cross the Atlantic and Arctic Ocean.

The map also shows the migratory route of the humpback whale. Its journey starts in the Arctic Ocean and continues along the coast of North America to southern California and northern Mexico. It is a trip of about 8,000 to 10,000 miles (13,000 to 16,000 kilometers).

Pps. 22–23, Biomes of the World

The map shows eight different biomes.

Biomes in the United States include: tundra, taiga, grassland, temperate forest, chaparral, and desert.

Major desert biomes are located in northern Africa, southwest and central Asia, and central Australia.

The three forest biomes are taiga forest, temperate forest, and rainforest. To visit a rainforest you would go to South America, Asia, and Africa.

Pps. 24–25, Searching for Gems

The chart should read:

Gold: South Africa, Russia, Canada, United States, Brazil

Silver: Mexico, Peru, Russia, United States, Canada, Australia

Diamonds: South Africa, India, Russia

Emeralds: Colombia, India, South Africa, Russia

Rubies: Myanmar, Sri Lanka, Thailand

Sapphires: India, Myanmar, Thailand, Sri Lanka, Australia

Opals: Australia, Europe, Mexico

You could find gold in South Africa, Russia, Canada, United States, and Brazil. You could find diamonds in South Africa, India, and Russia.

In Thailand, you would find rubies and sapphires.

Pps. 26–27, Where In the World?

1. North America, Mexico

2. South America, Colombia

3. Africa, Somalia

4. Asia, Mongolia

5. Europe, Spain

6. Asia, Iran

Glossary

biome A major area of the Earth with a certain kind of climate and certain kinds of plants and animals.

border The boundary of a state or country.

climate The weather of a place over a long period of time.

continent One of seven great land masses on the Earth.

crust The solid outer layer of the Earth's surface.

equator An imaginary line that separates the Earth into the Northern and Southern hemispheres.

map key A list that explains the meaning of the symbols used on a map.

migration Large numbers of animals moving from one place to another.

natural resource A product that comes from the Earth.

Pangaea The name of the large landmass that was Earth about 180 miliion years ago.

plain A large flat stretch of land.

taiga An evergreen forest in an arctic region with a cold polar climate.

tundra A treeless, harsh grassland with very short cool summers and long cold winters.

tectonic plates Sections of the Earth's crust that float on the Earth's molten, outer core.

temperature How hot or cold something is.

Index